DavidLanz.com
Amariemusic.com

Original cover art by Martin Springett
www.martinspringett.com

Music editing by Kathy Parsons
mainlypiano.com

ISBN 978-1-4950-2349-1

In Australia Contact:
Hal Leonard Australia Pty. Ltd.
4 Lentara Court
Cheltenham, Victoria, 3192 Australia
Email: ausadmin@halleonard.com.au

Visit Hal Leonard Online at
www.halleonard.com

WINTER'S PRELUDE

By DAVID LANZ
and KRISTIN M. LANZ

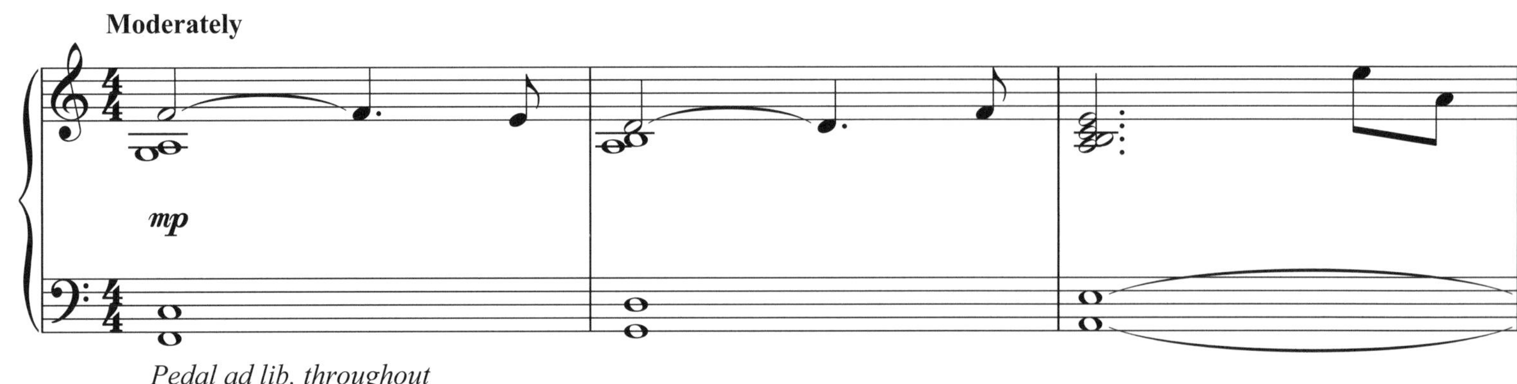

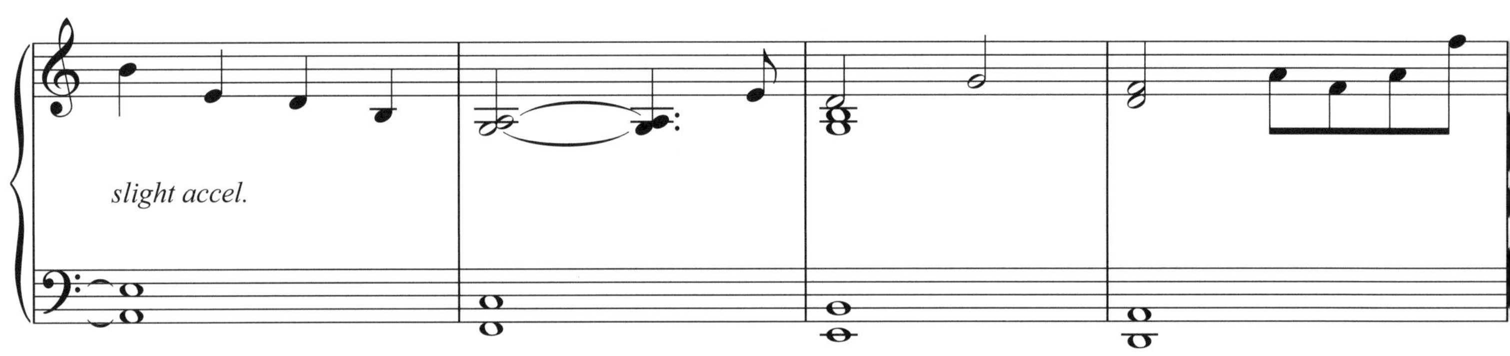

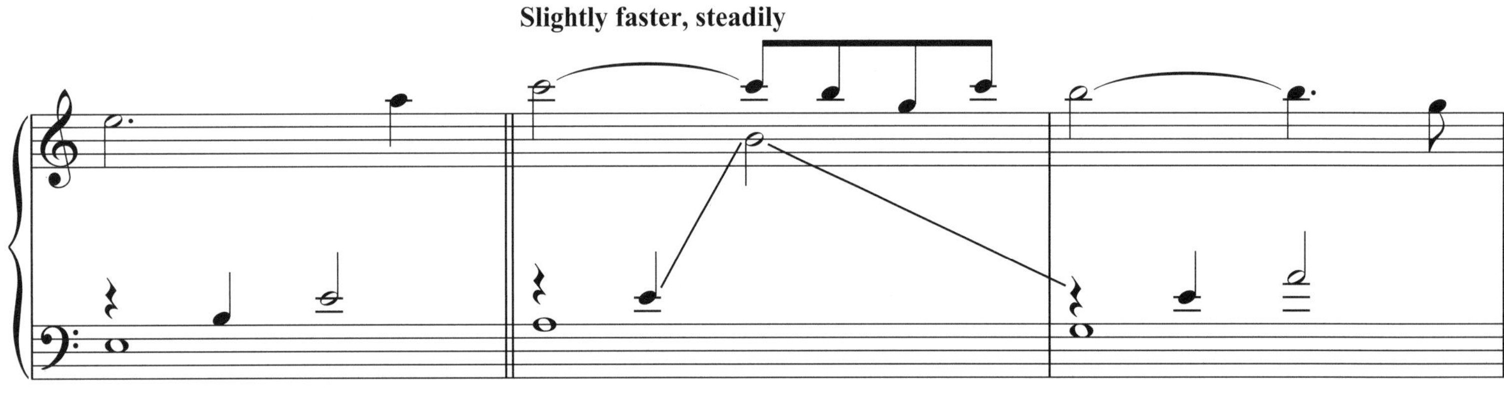

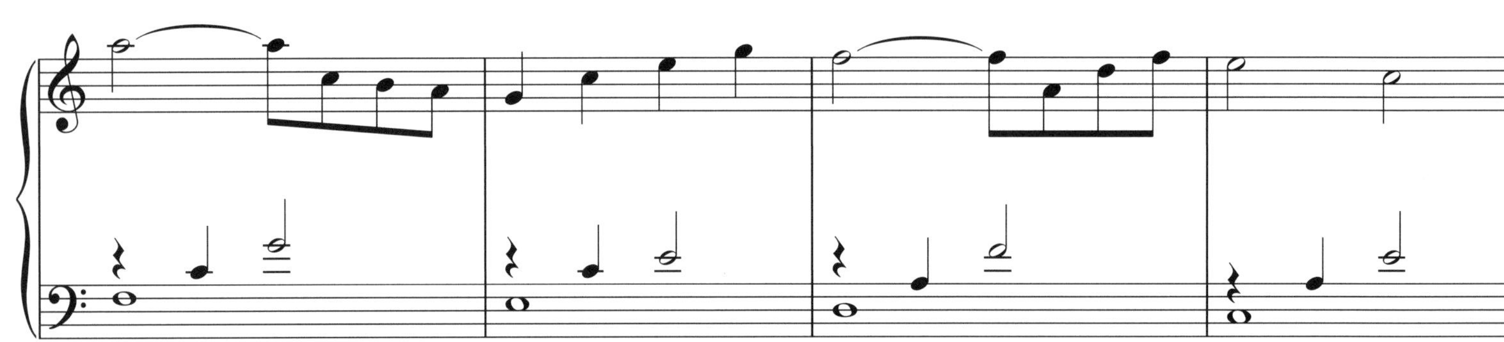

3

rit.

a tempo

rit.

FOREVER CHRISTMAS

By DAVID LANZ
and KRISTIN M. LANZ

*Lead vocal written one octave higher than sung.

D♭
C
Fm
Cm
true?
For - ev - er
Christ - mas,
E♭m7
A♭9sus
D♭
A♭
Fm
peace on earth, let there be love for me and
B♭7sus
B♭
E♭sus
E♭
you.
With
A♭(add2)
Cm
D♭
E♭/D♭
D♭
friends and fam - i - ly gath - ered 'round to

A♭ Cm D♭ C
ring in an - oth - er new year, to -
Fm Fm/B♭ Cm7 E♭m7 A♭9sus D♭(add2)
night the world, with all its woes, fades a -
A♭ Fm B♭m E♭9sus A♭sus
way like a dream we'll speak not of.
A♭ D♭
Feel the warmth of
mf

Cm
Db
Eb9sus
Christ - mas, a time for all hearts to be
8va
Abmaj7
Ab(add2)
Fbmaj7
Fbmaj7/Gb
light. Stay a while; let's
Cbmaj7
Abm7
Bb7sus
Fb
see your smile, feel the joy all through the
Eb7sus
Eb
Fm
Gm
Ab(add2)
Cm
night. We'll sing, and we'll re -

D♭
A♭
Cm
mem - ber the day when Christ - mas first
D♭
C
Fm
Cm7
dawned. And hearts will break when
E♭m7
A♭9sus
D♭
A♭
Fm
we re - call those we love, but now are
B♭m7
E♭sus
A♭(add2)
Cm
gone, they're gone.
mf

D♭
A♭(add2)
Cm
D♭
A♭/C
Fm
Cm
E♭m
A♭7
D♭(add2)
A♭(add2)
Fm
B♭m7
E♭sus
A♭sus
f
A♭
D♭
D♭(add2)
Feel the warmth of
mp

Cm
D♭
E♭9sus
Christ - mas, a time for all hearts to be
8va
mp
A♭(add2)
A♭maj7
F♭maj7
A♭m/G♭
light. Stay a while; let's
C♭maj7
A♭m9
B♭m11
see your smile, feel the joy all through the
E♭7sus
night. What
p
poco rit.
pp

A♭(add2)
Cm7
D♭(add2)
would I wish for all year long, if
a tempo
mp
A♭(add2)
Cm
D♭
C
dreams real - ly did come true? For -
mf
Fm
Cm7
E♭m7
A♭9sus
D♭
ev - er Christ - mas; peace on earth; on - ly
mp
A♭
Fm7
Gm7♭5
C
love for me and you. For -
mf
mp

Fm
Cm
E♭m7
A♭9sus
D♭
ev - er
Christ - mas;
peace
on
earth;
let there
A♭
Fm
be
on - ly
love
for
B♭7sus
B♭
E♭sus
E♭
A♭(add2)
each
and
ev - 'ry - one.
Cm
D♭
E♭sus
A♭(add2)
rit.

JUBILATE

By DAVID LANZ
and KRISTIN M. LANZ

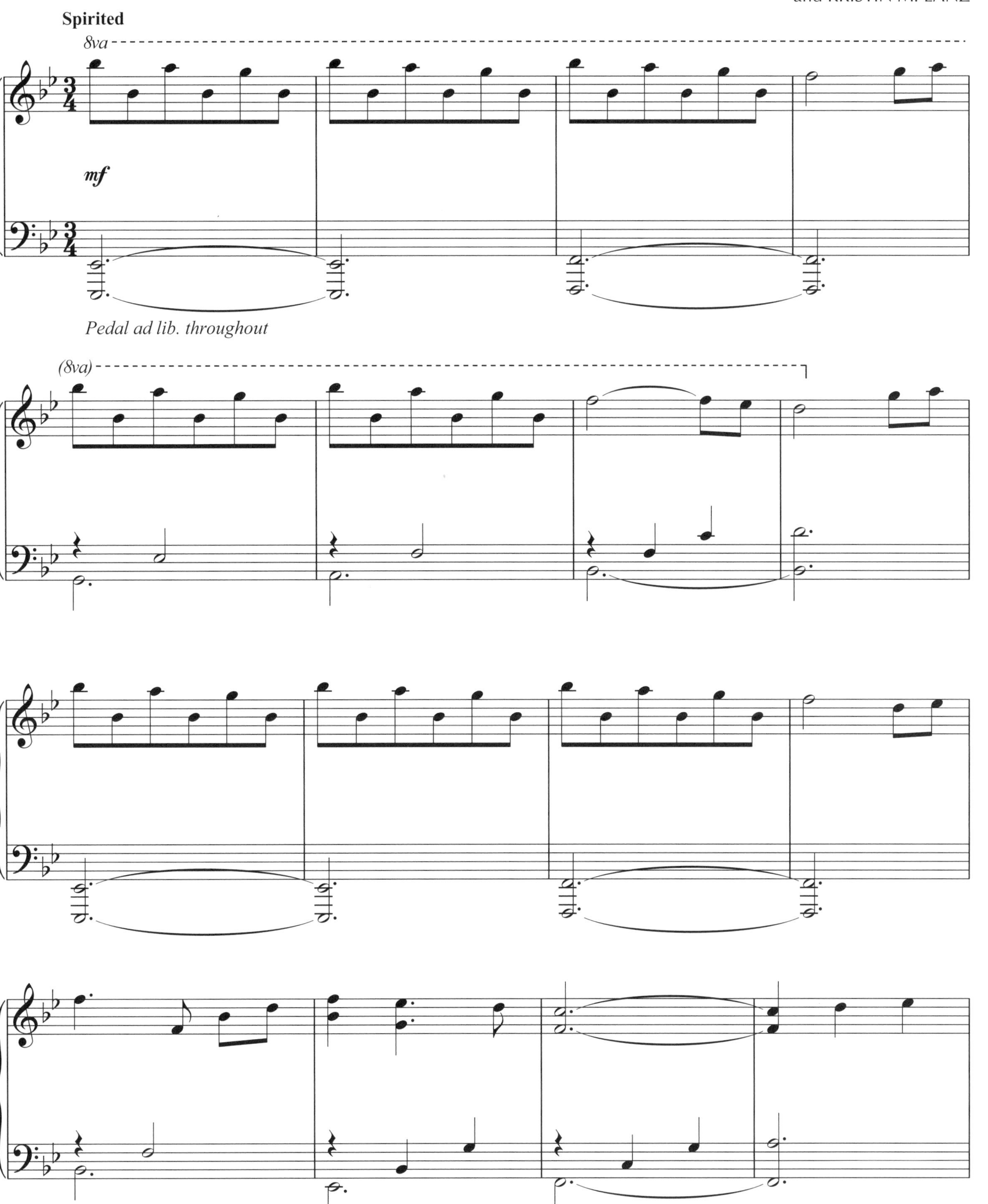

f

mf

mp
mf
mp

Slightly slower
rit.
Slower

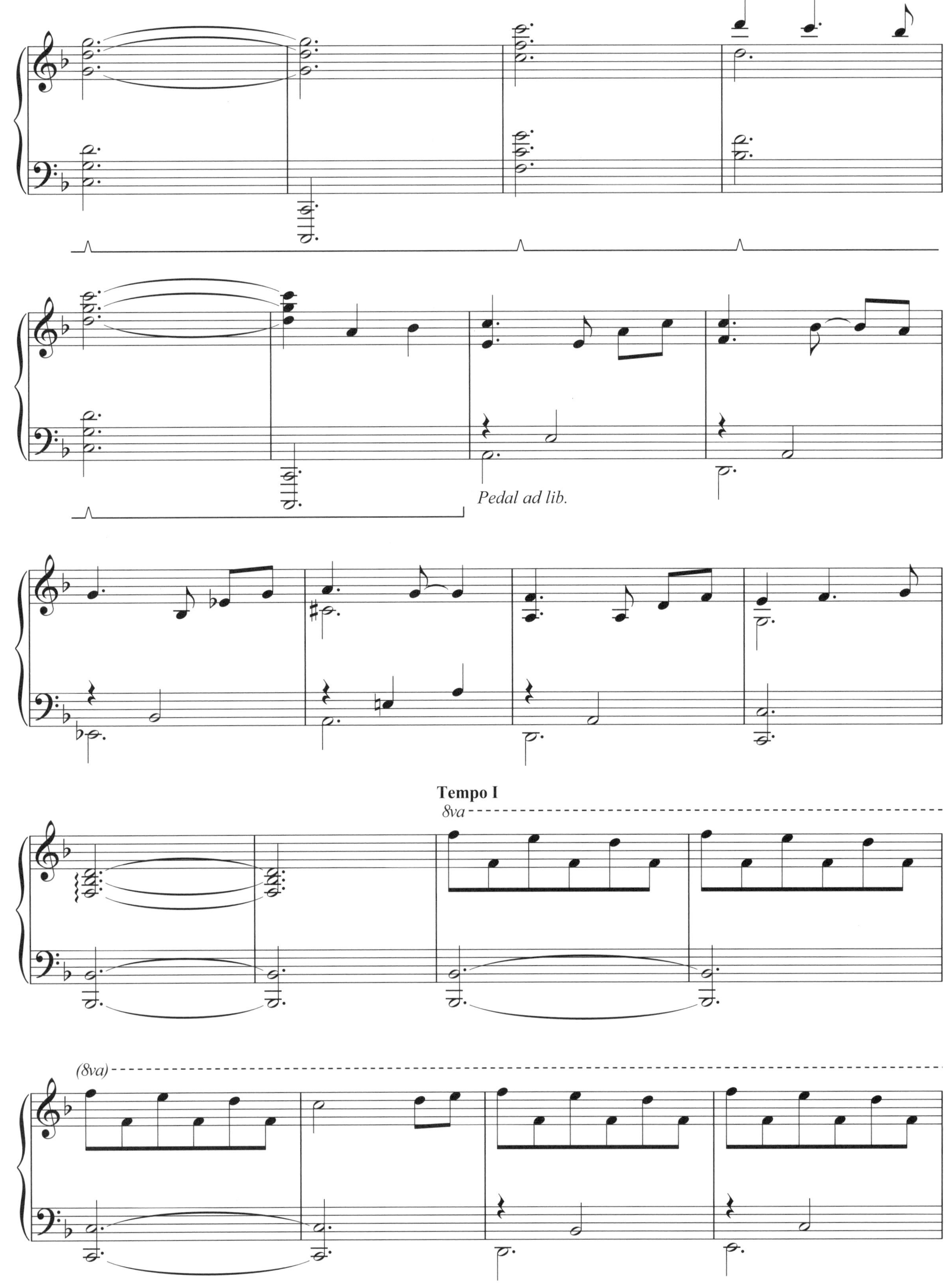
Pedal ad lib.
Tempo I
8va
(8va)

(8va)
rit.
8vb
(8vb)
8va
poco rit.
f

SNOW DANCE

By DAVID LANZ
and KRISTIN M. LANZ

rit.
pp
a tempo
p
rit.

OH HOLY NIGHT

By ADOLPHE ADAM
Arranged by DAVID LANZ and KRISTIN M. LANZ

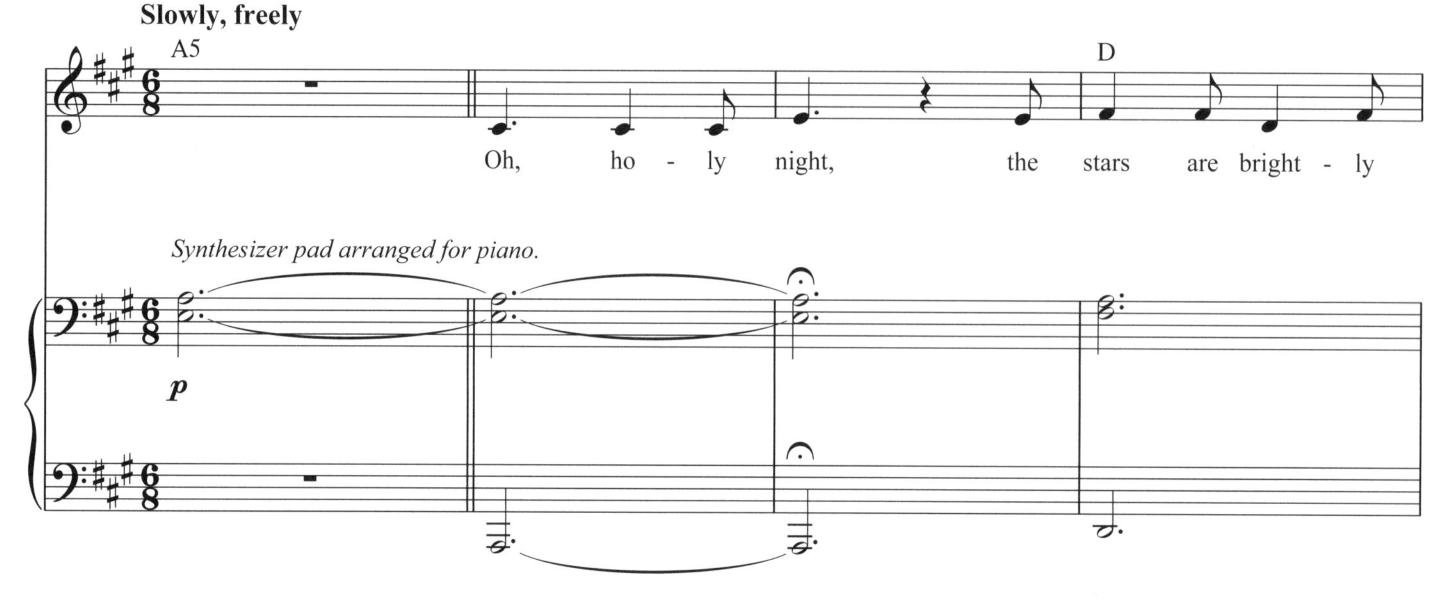

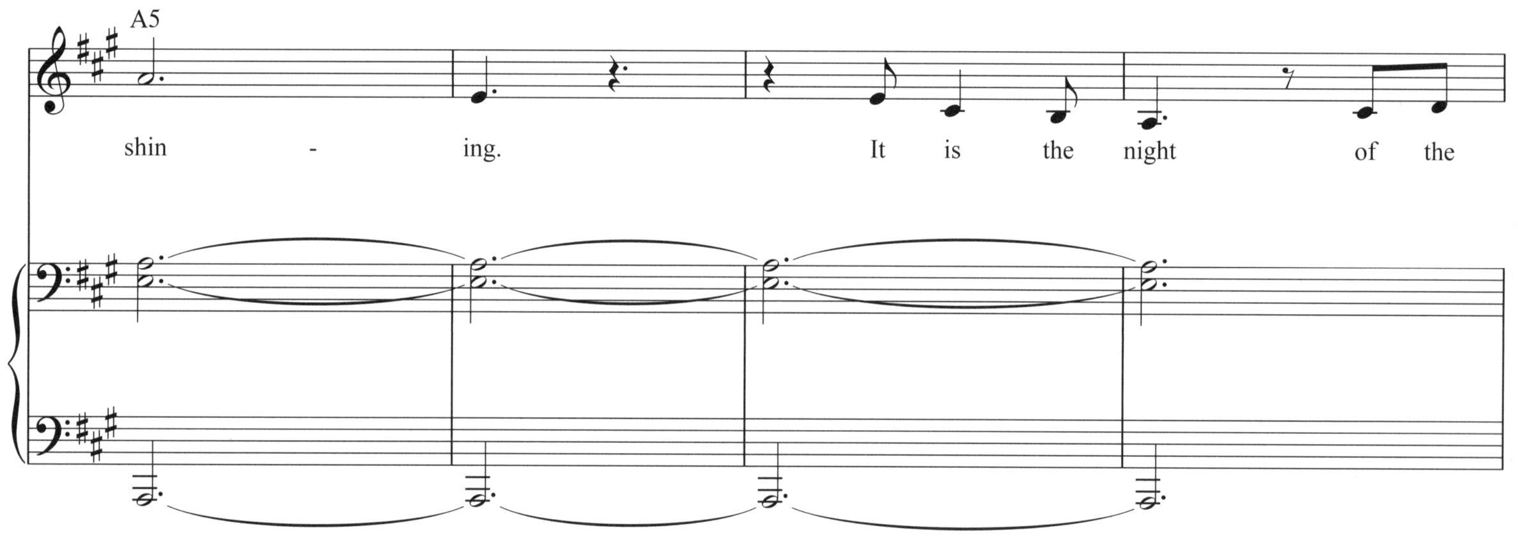

D
Long lay the world, in sin and er - ror
A
G♯
C♯m
G♯
pin - ing, 'til He ap - peared, and the soul felt its
C♯m
E
worth. A thrill of hope. The
A
E
wear - y world re - joic - es, for yon - der breaks a

A
F♯m
new and glor - ious morn.
Fall
on your
mf
C♯m
Bm
E7/G♯
knees.
Oh, hear
the an - gel
F♯m
A
E/G♯
voic - es.
Oh, night
di-
f
p
F♯m
D
A
E
vine,
oh, night when Christ
was

A
E
E/G♯
born.
Oh,
night
di -
mf
f
A
A/C♯
D
vine.
Oh,
8vb
A
E
A
night,
oh,
night
di - vine.
p
mp
mf

D
A
E
A
Chains shall He
mp
break, for the slave is our broth - er; and in His
D
A
G♯
8va
C♯m
G♯
C♯m
name, all op - pres - sion shall cease.
Sweet

E
A
hymns of joy in grate - ful chor - us raise we. Let
E
A
all with - in us praise His ho - ly name.
f
F♯m
C♯m
Christ is the Lord! Let
Bm
E7
F♯m
ev - er, ev - er praise Thee. No -
mf

A
E/G♯
F♯m
D
el! Ɩ No - el! Oh, ho - ly
A
E
A
night, oh, night Ɩ di - vine. No -
f
E
E/G♯
A
A/C♯
D
el! Ɩ No - el! Ɩ Oh,
rit.
mp
a tempo
8vb
A
E
A
night, oh, night Ɩ di - vine. Ɩ No -

E
E/G♯
A
A/C♯
D
el!
No - el!
f
8vb
N.C.
A
N.C.
Oh, night,
oh,
Synthesizer pad arranged for piano.
pp
(8vb)
E5
A
ho - ly
night.
Piano as recorded
mp
rit.

LA ESTRELLA DE LA NAVIDAD

By DAVID LANZ
and KRISTIN M. LANZ

mp
8va
p
rit.
pp

SWEET WINTER LOVE

By DAVID LANZ
and KRISTIN M. LANZ

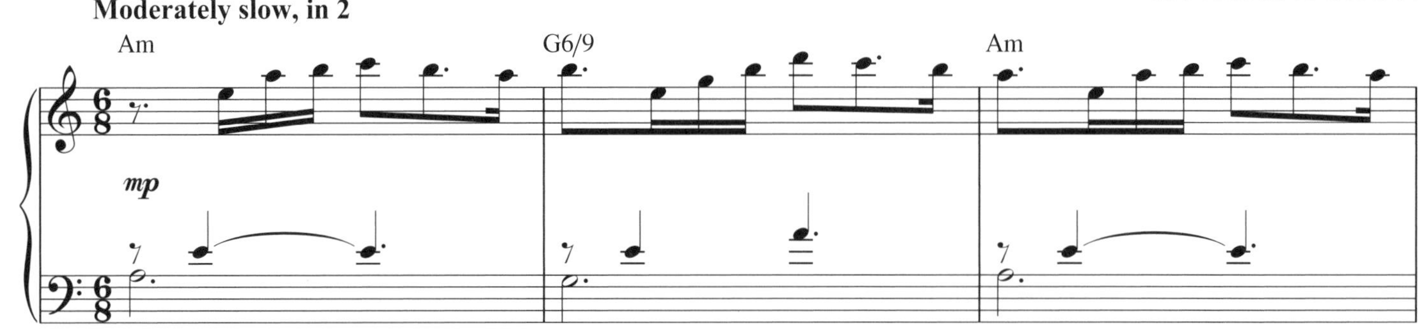

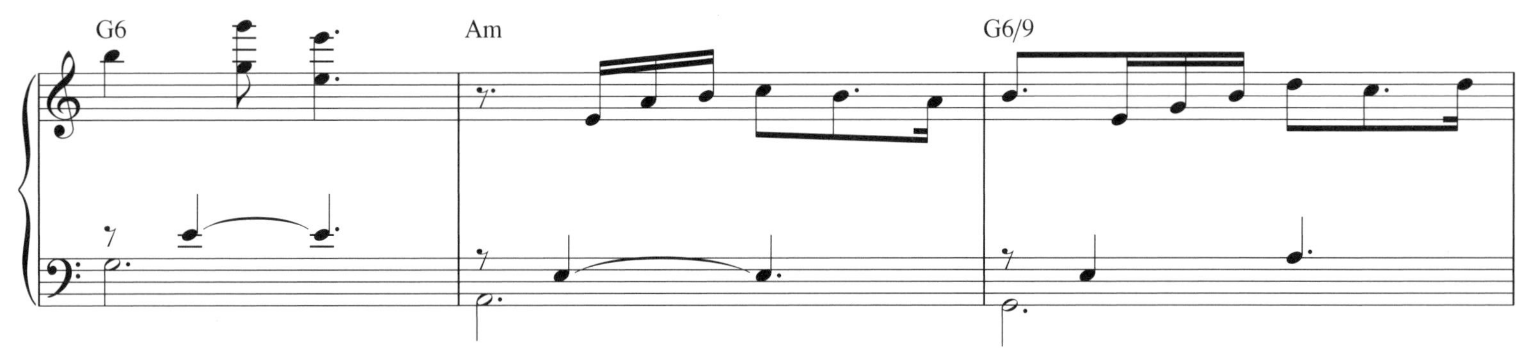

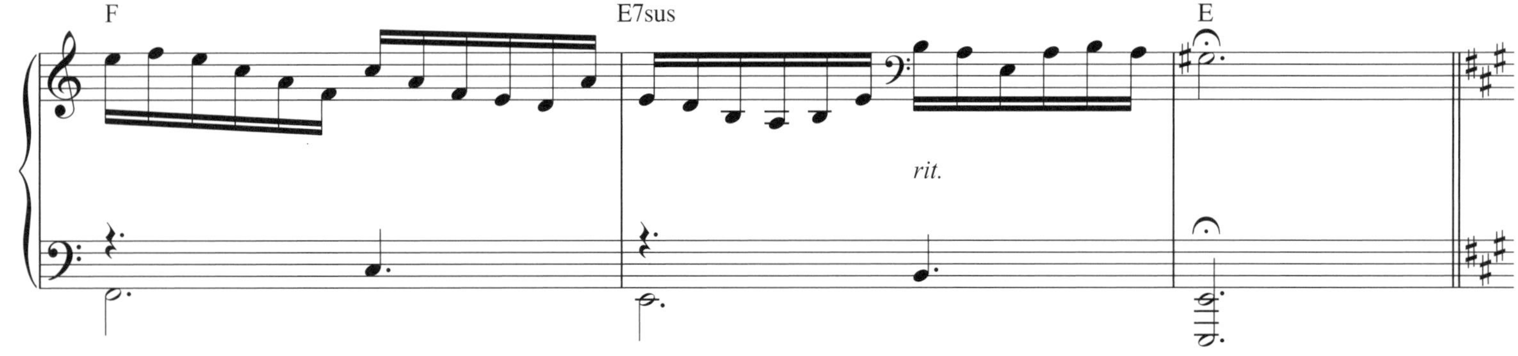

G D A D E
soar - ing. Yule fire roar - ing in -
8vb
F♯sus F♯ Am
- side. Bright Christ - mas
(8vb)
D E A G D
sun - shine shines on the sky - line.
A D E F♯sus
Bril - liant, and so fine out - side.

F#
D
A
On Christ - mas morn - ing,
D
A
F
love fills the air: white win - ter
C
Esus
E7sus
Esus
days, ic - y blue nights.
E
A
Dur - ing this
mf
mp

D
E
A
G
D
Yule - tide, joy - ful - ness can't hide,
A
D
E
F♯sus
keep - ing us warm and so light.
F♯
D
A
On Christ - mas morn - ing,
D
A
F
love filled the air. I gave you my

C Esus E Am
heart on Christ - mas day. Can - dy cane
rit.
a tempo
D9 G Cmaj9
kiss - es for you; sweet win - ter love shin - ing
F Dm E7sus
through; mis - tle - toe dreams all com - ing true.
E F♯m7 E/G♯ Am D9
Su - gar plums dance to the

G
Cmaj9
F
tune; gin - ger - bread man in the moon: yes, we be -
Dm7
Esus
E
lieve it's Christ - mas time.
8vb
Lightly
Am
G6/9
Am
G6
Am
G6/9

Fmaj7
E7sus
E
A
On Christ - mas
mf
D
E
A
G
D
morn - ing, an - gels were soar - ing.
8vb
A
D
E
F♯5
Yule fire roar - ing in - side.
F♯
D
A
Dur - ing this Yule - tide,
mp

D
A
D
love filled the air.
You gave me your
A
B7sus
E
heart on Christ - mas day.
f
D
A
D
On Christ - mas morn - ing,
love filled the
mf
A
F
C
Esus
air.
I gave you my heart on Christ - mas day,
rit.
mp

E
Am
G6/9
on Christ - mas
day.
a tempo
Am
G6
Am
On Christ - mas
day.
G6/9
Fmaj7
Dm9
Fmaj7
Asus
A
rit.

WHAT IS CHRISTMAS?

By DAVID LANZ
and KRISTIN M. LANZ

Moderately, expressively

Fmaj7 Gm7 Am Bbm7

mp *rit.*

F Dm G7 C9sus

a tempo *rit.*

What is

F Em7b5 A7#5 Dm7 Bbmaj7

a tempo

Christ - mas? Do you know? Love - ly gifts and fall - ing snow, San - ta's

F Eb Dm G7sus

rit.

laugh - ter Christ - mas Eve, sing - ing car - ols 'round the tree.

*Lead vocal written one octave higher than sung.

C9sus
F
Em7♭5
A7♯5
Dm7
"Peace on Earth," you may say: it's the rea - son to -
a tempo
B♭maj7
F
E♭
Dm
day. Why just one day of the year, and the rest wrapped in
G7sus
C9sus
Fmaj7
Gm7
fear? Tell me now, tell me true: what does
rit.
a tempo
Am
B♭m
F
Dm
Christ - mas mean to you? Does it fill your heart with won - der, or

G7
C7sus
Fmaj7
Gm7
leave you blue? Tell me, please, tell me why all the
Am
B♭m7
F
Dm
an - gels in the sky, when they look down on us, why
rit.
a tempo
G7
C9sus
B♭/F
F
do they cry? All the
A♭maj7
Fmaj7
things we hold so dear, bring - ing

A♭maj7
Fmaj7
sights and sounds of cheer: are they
Dm
Am
Christ - mas? Tell me true, what does
E♭maj7
C9
Christ - mas mean, mean to you? Find the
Fmaj7
Gm7
Am
B♭m
star in your heart; this is where Christ - mas starts. Feel the
rit.

F Dm7 G7 C7sus
light gent - ly glow; feel your love play its part. Tell me
a tempo
Fmaj7 Gm7 Am B♭m7
now, tell me true, what is Christ - mas to you? Peace with -
rit.
F Dm G7 C9sus
in: do you see? That's what Christ - mas means
a tempo
rit.
F E♭6 Fsus F E♭maj7 F5
to me.
a tempo
3
rit.

WINTER STAR

By DAVID LANZ
and KRISTIN M. LANZ

8va
mp
Pedal ad lib. throughout
(8va)
(8va)
(8va)
mp

mf
mf

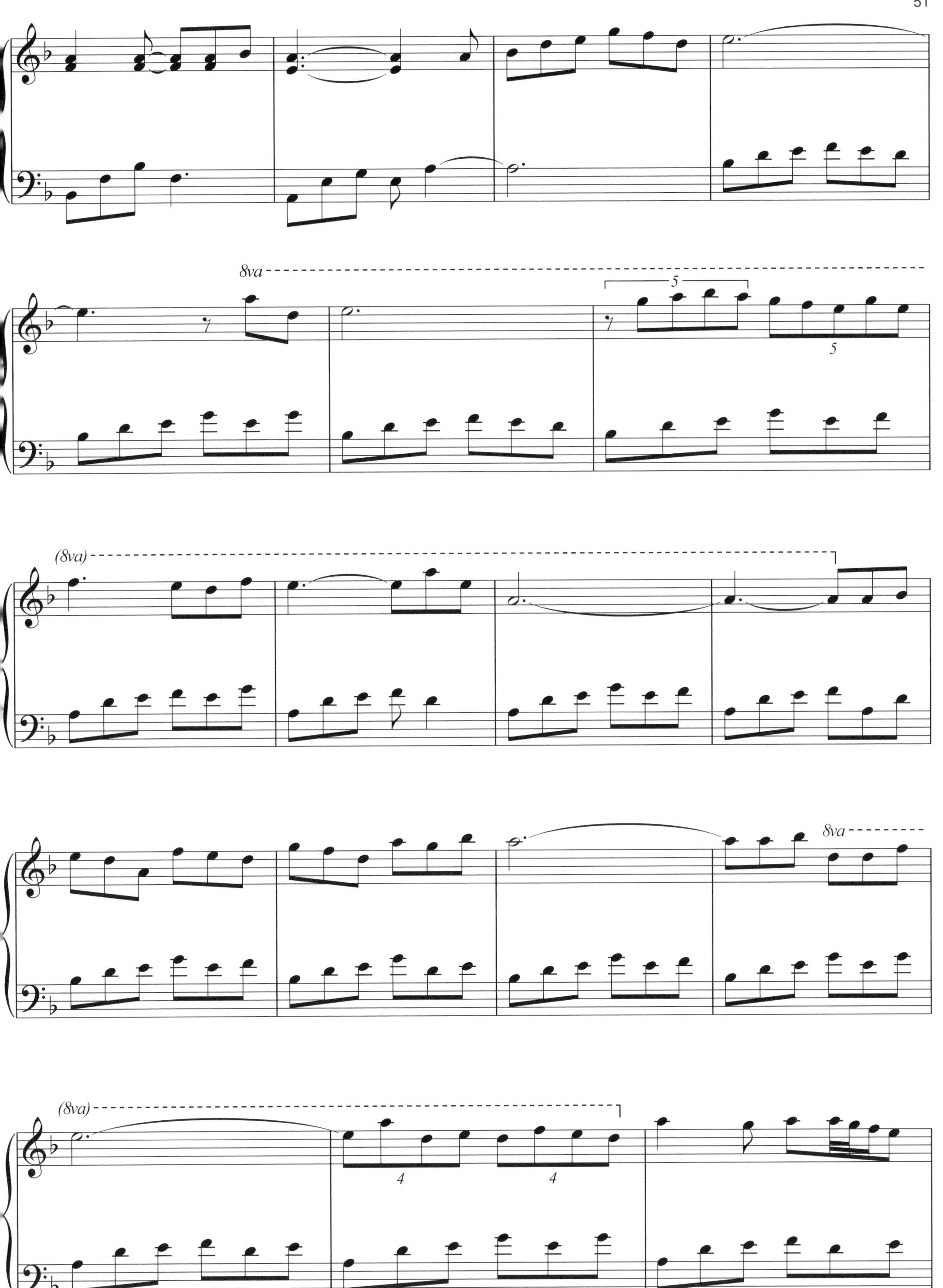
8va
5
5
(8va)
8va
(8va)
4
4

mp
8va
p
(8va)
(8va)
8va
rit.
pp

A THOUSAND LIGHTS

Arranged by DAVID LANZ
and KRISTIN M. LANZ

F
A7♭9
Dm
B♭(add2)
C
heav - en's stars spread out their love to bless the Sav - ior's
F
A7♭9
Dm
B♭(add2)
birth.
C
Fsus
F
C/E
Nu tän - das tu - sen
Dm
Am
B♭
G
C
ju - lel - jus på jor - dens mör - ka rund, och

F
A
Dm
B♭(add2)
C
tu - sen, tu - sen strå - la ock på him - lens djup - blå
rit.
a tempo
F
C/E
Dm
Am
grund.
mf
3
B♭
G
C
F
A
Dm
B♭(add2)
C
Fsus
F
Och

C/E
Dm
Am
B♭
G
ö - ver stad och land i kväll går ju - lens gla - da
mp
C
F
A7♭9
Dm
B♭(add2)
bud, att född är Her - ren Je - sus Krist, vår
C
Dm
B♭m7
E♭
Fräl - sa - re och Gud.
A
A♭
E♭/G
Fm
Cm
thou - sand lights are lit to - night; they

D♭
B♭7
E♭
A♭
C
bright - en up our earth. And stars from heav - en
Fm(add2)
D♭
E♭
spread their love. Re - joice!
p
8vb
Fm
Our Sav - ior's birth!
(8vb)
Pedal ad lib.
D♭
A♭
A♭sus
A♭
rit.

SILENT NIGHT

By FRANZ GRUBER and JOSEPH MOHR
Arranged by DAVID LANZ and KRISTIN M. LANZ

F
All is calm,
E♭
B♭
all is bright
E♭
F/E♭
E♭
'round yon vir - gin
B♭
Gm
moth - er and child,

E♭
ho - ly in - fant so
B♭(add2)
ten - der and mild.
Gm
F
Sleep in heav - en - ly
D7♭9/F♯
Gm
Em7♭5
peace.

B♭
Fsus2
F
Sleep
in
heav - en - ly
B♭
Gm
B♭
Gm
peace.
B♭
Gm
B♭
Gm
B♭(add2)
Gm(add2)
Stil - le Nacht,

B♭(add2)
Gm(add2)
hei - li - ge Nacht,
F
Al - les schläft;
E♭
B♭5
B♭sus
B♭
ein - sam wacht.
E♭
F/E♭
E♭
Nur das trau - te hoch -

B♭(add2)
Gm
hei - li - ge Paar.
E♭
Hol - der Kna - be im
B♭(add2)
Gm
lock - i - gen Haar,
F
D7♭9/F♯
Schlaf in himm - li - scher

Gm
Em7♭5
Ruh!
B♭(add2)
F
Schlaf
in
himm - li - scher
B♭
Gm
Ruh!
mf
B♭sus2
Gm
3

F
E♭
B♭5
B♭7
E♭
F/E♭
E♭
p
B♭
mp
Gm
mf
E♭
F/E♭
E♭

B♭sus2
Gm
mp
F
D7♭9/F♯
mf
Gm
Em7♭5
p
B♭
F
mp
B♭
Gm
B♭
Gm

B♭
Gm
B♭
Gm
Very slowly, freely
Tempo I
B♭
Gm
B♭
Gm
Si - lent night.
Ho - ly night.
mf
F
Fsus
F
All is calm,
E♭
B♭5
B♭
all is bright

E♭
F/E♭
E♭
'round yon vir - gin
B♭
Gm
moth - er and child,
E♭
F/E♭
E♭
ho - ly in - fant so
B♭(add2)
Gm
ten - der and mild.

F
D7♭9/F♯
Sleep in heav - en - ly
Gm
Em7♭5
peace.
rit.
Slowly, freely
B♭sus2
F
E♭
Sleep in heav - en - ly peace.
p
8vb
B♭
rit.
8va
(8vb)

HEAVENLY PEACE

By DAVID LANZ
and KRISTIN M. LANZ

8va
3